THIS BOOK

BELONGS TO

○○○

COLOR TEST

WHEELS

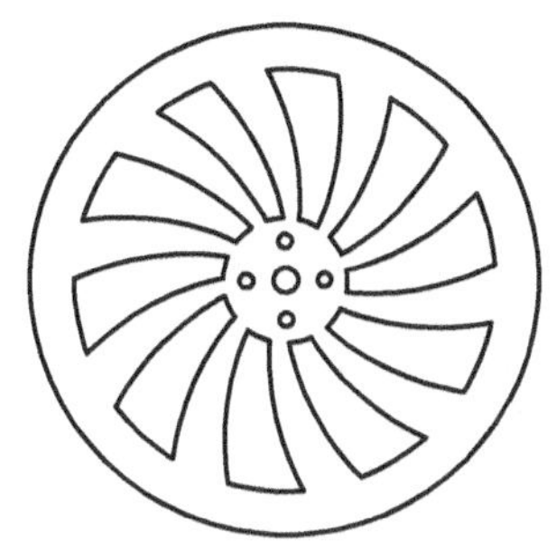

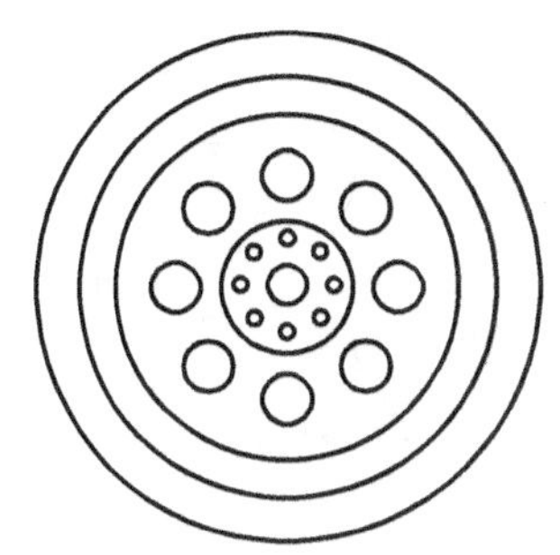

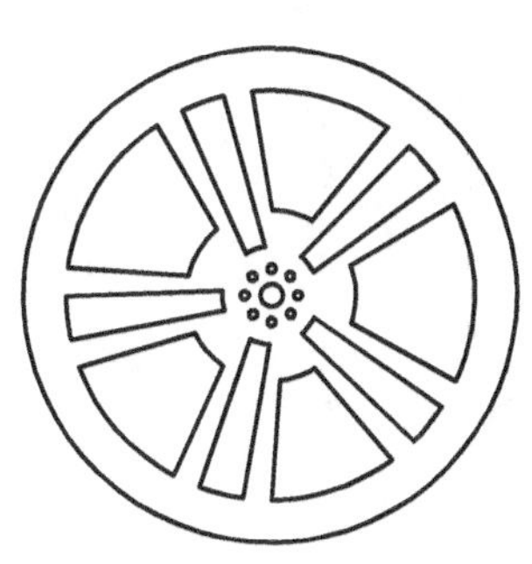

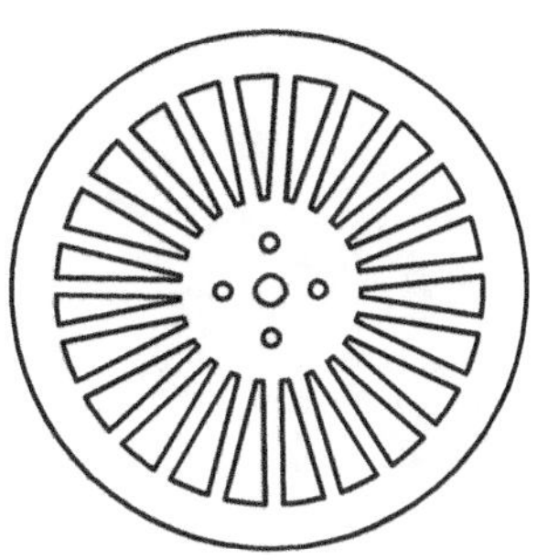

 # REPEAT 

 # REPEAT 

 # REPEAT 

 # REPEAT 

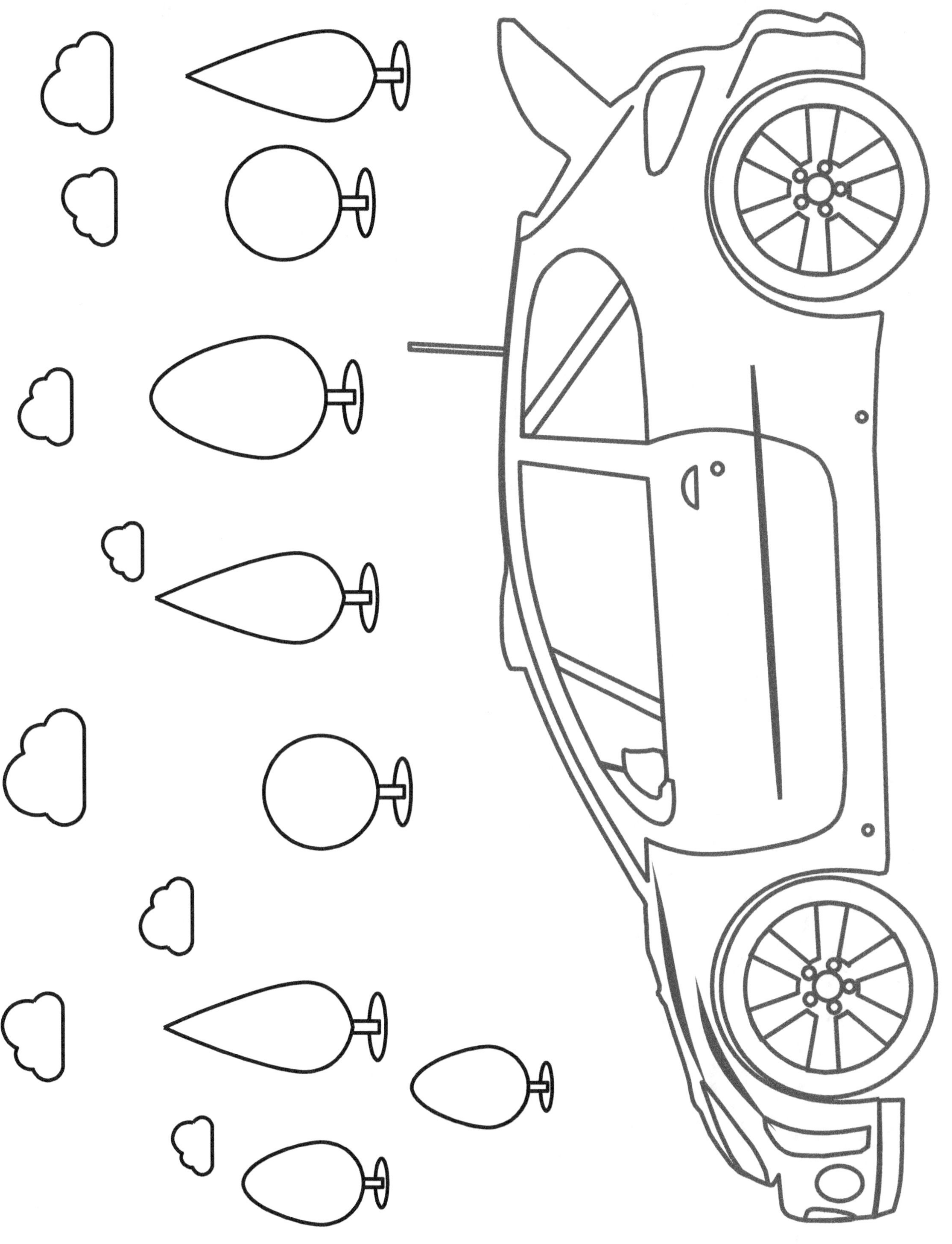

 # REPEAT 

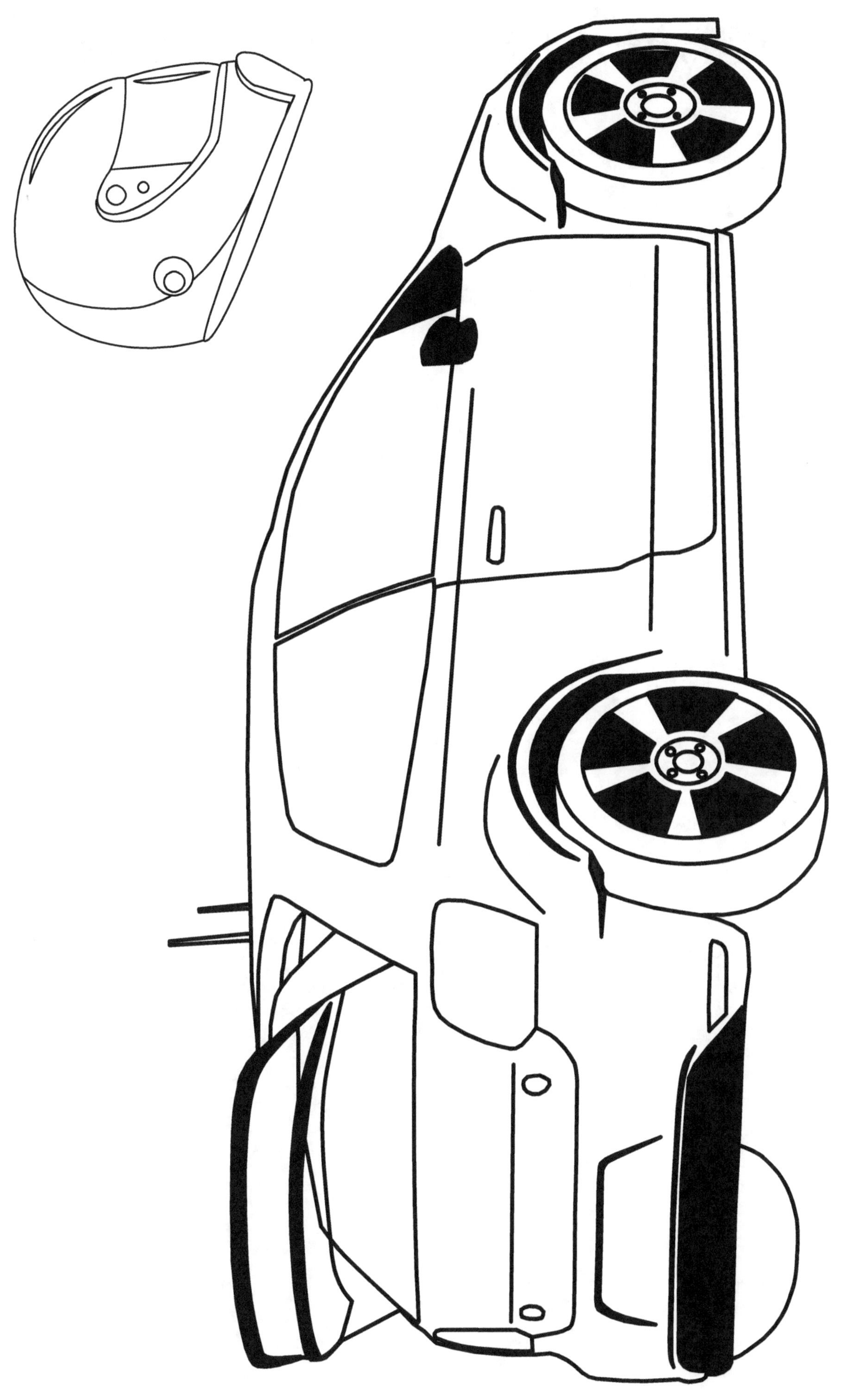

 # REPEAT 

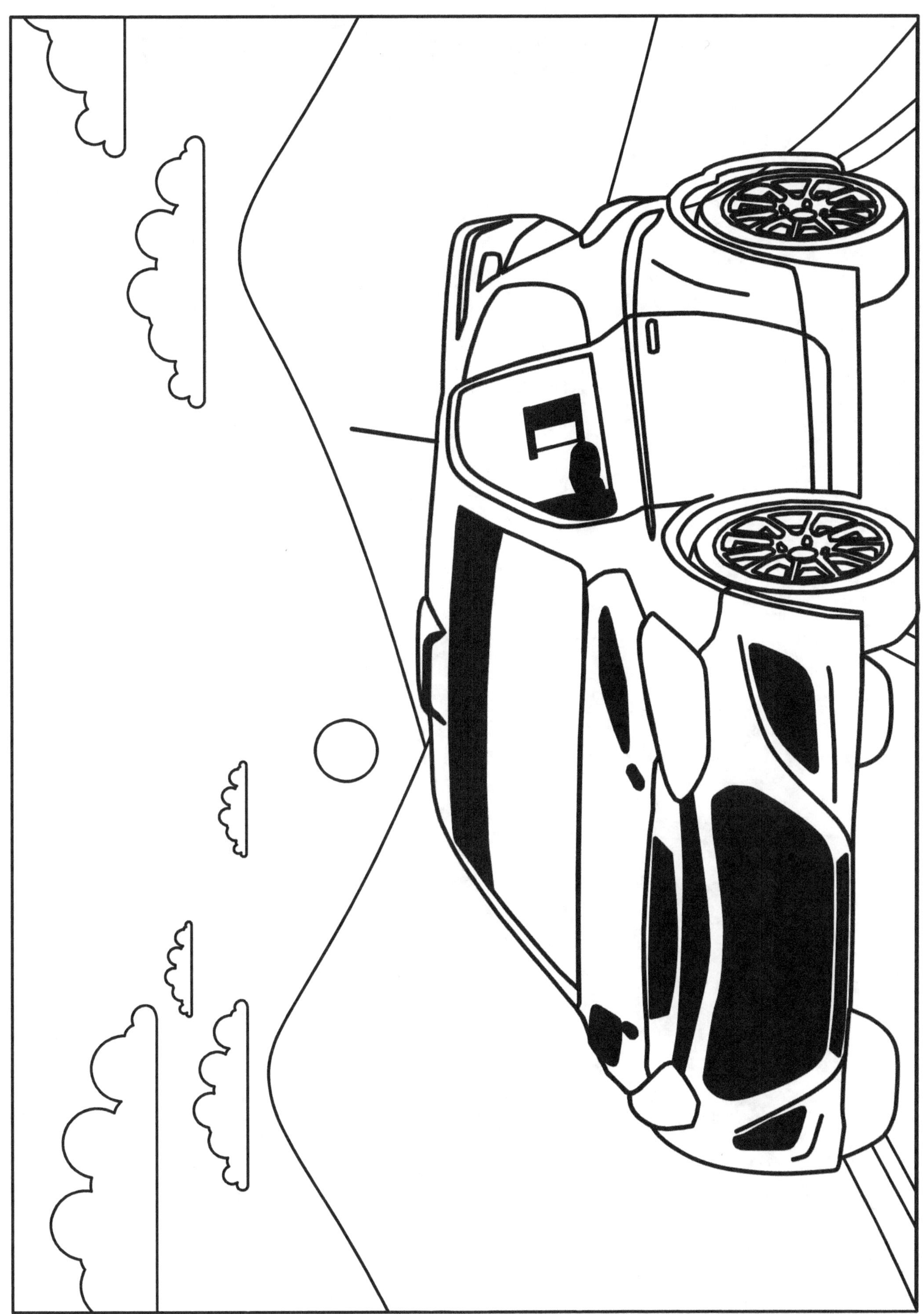

 # REPEAT 

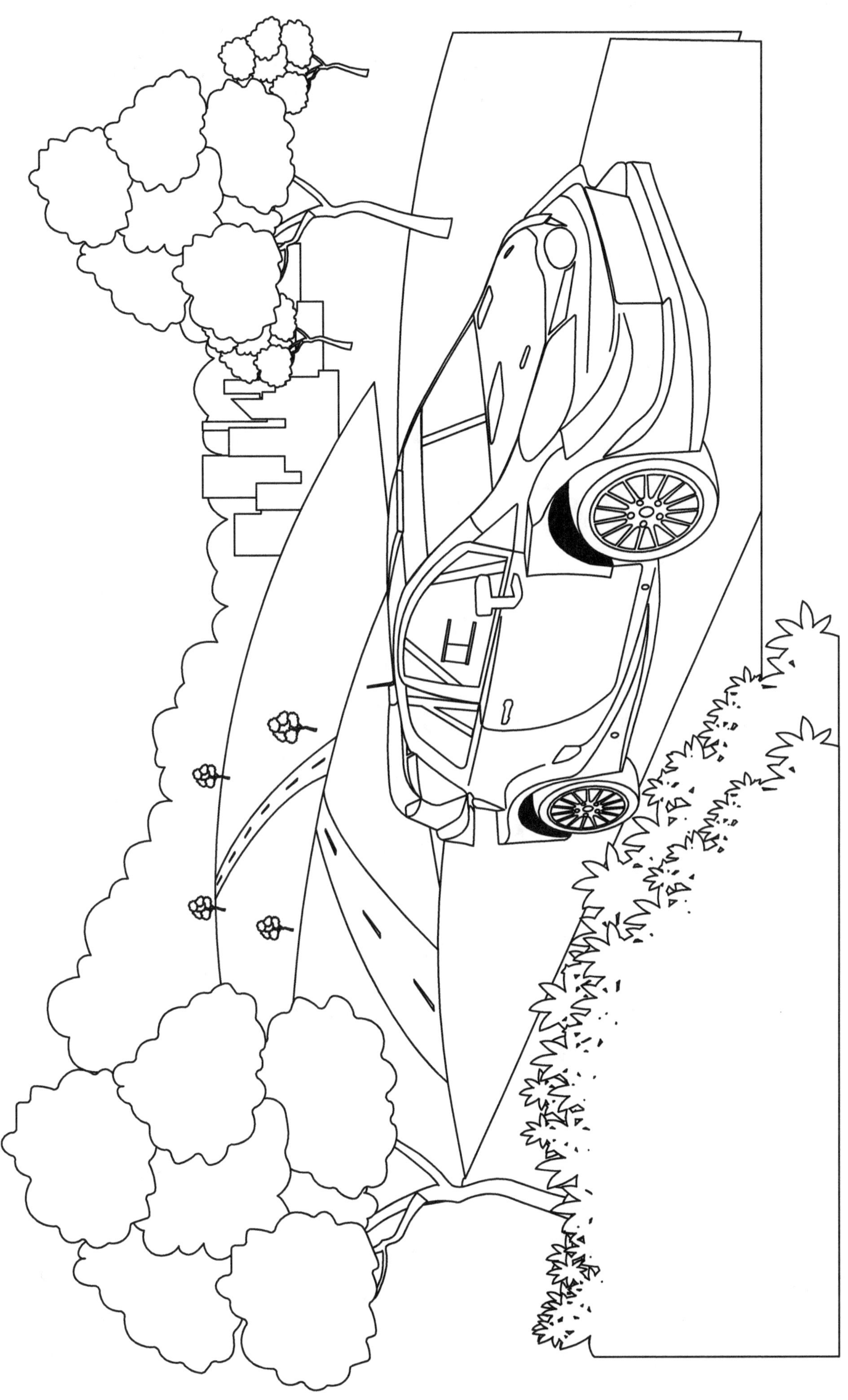

 # REPEAT 

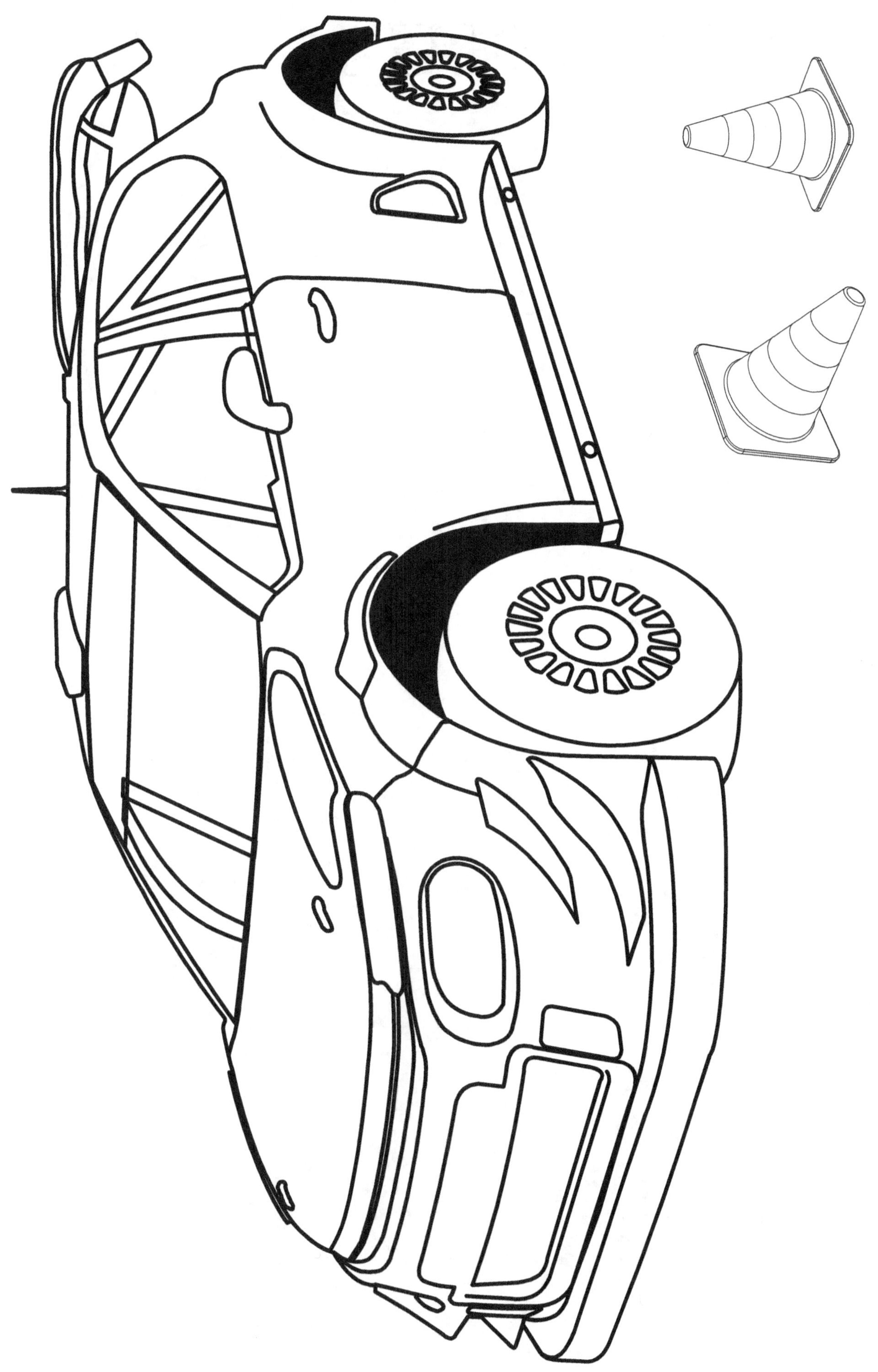

 # REPEAT 

 # REPEAT 

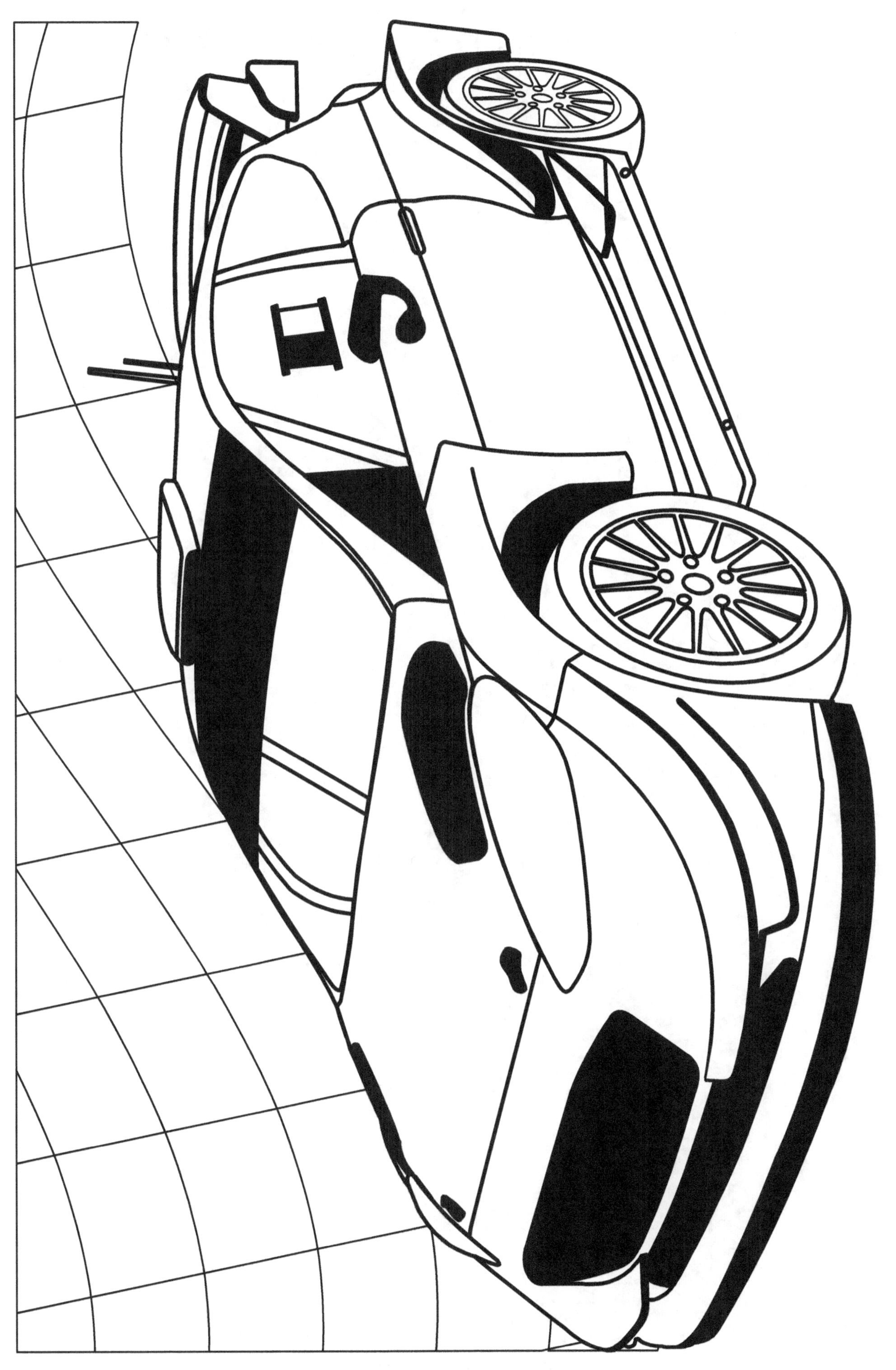

 # REPEAT 

 # REPEAT 

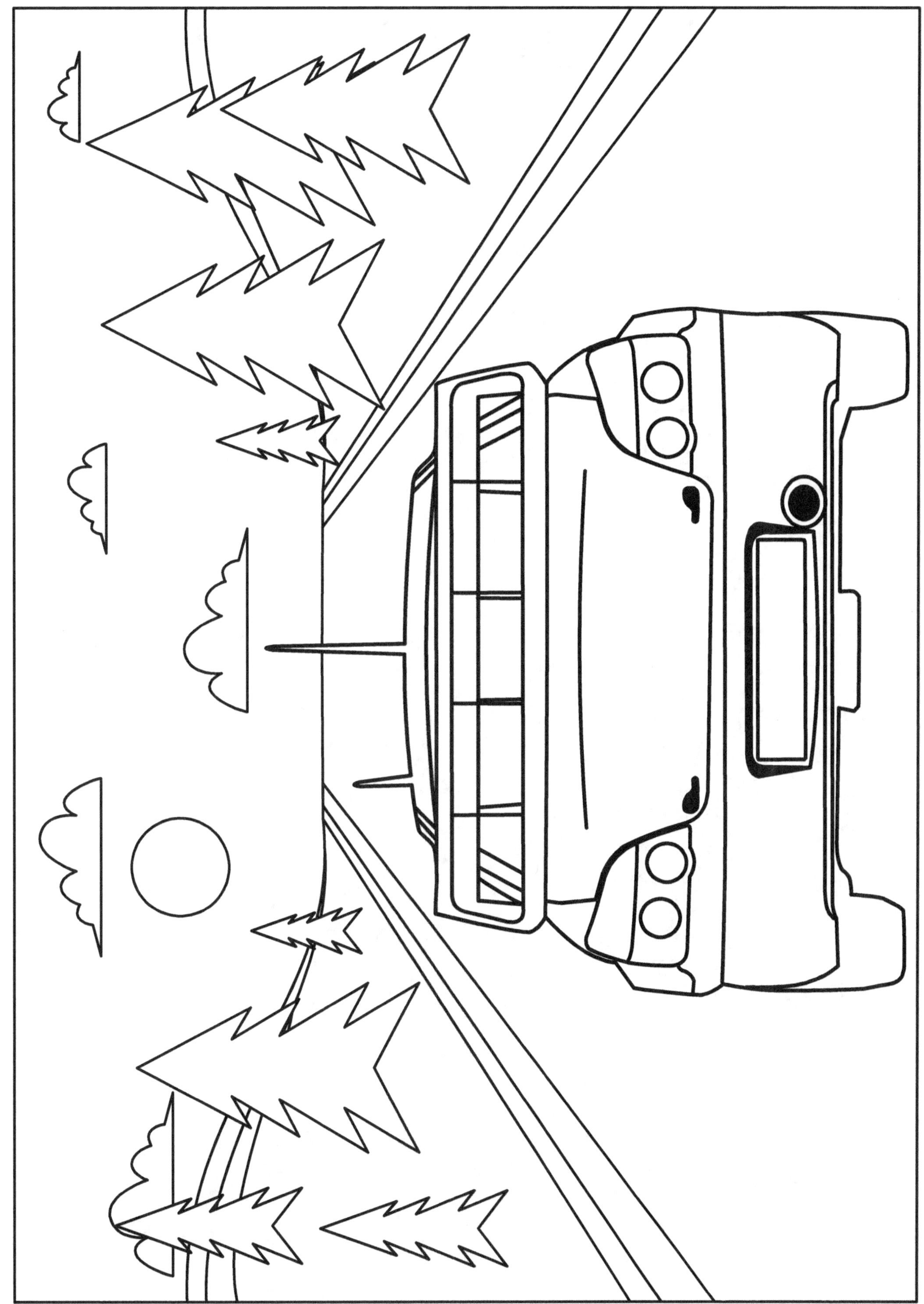

 # REPEAT 

 # REPEAT 

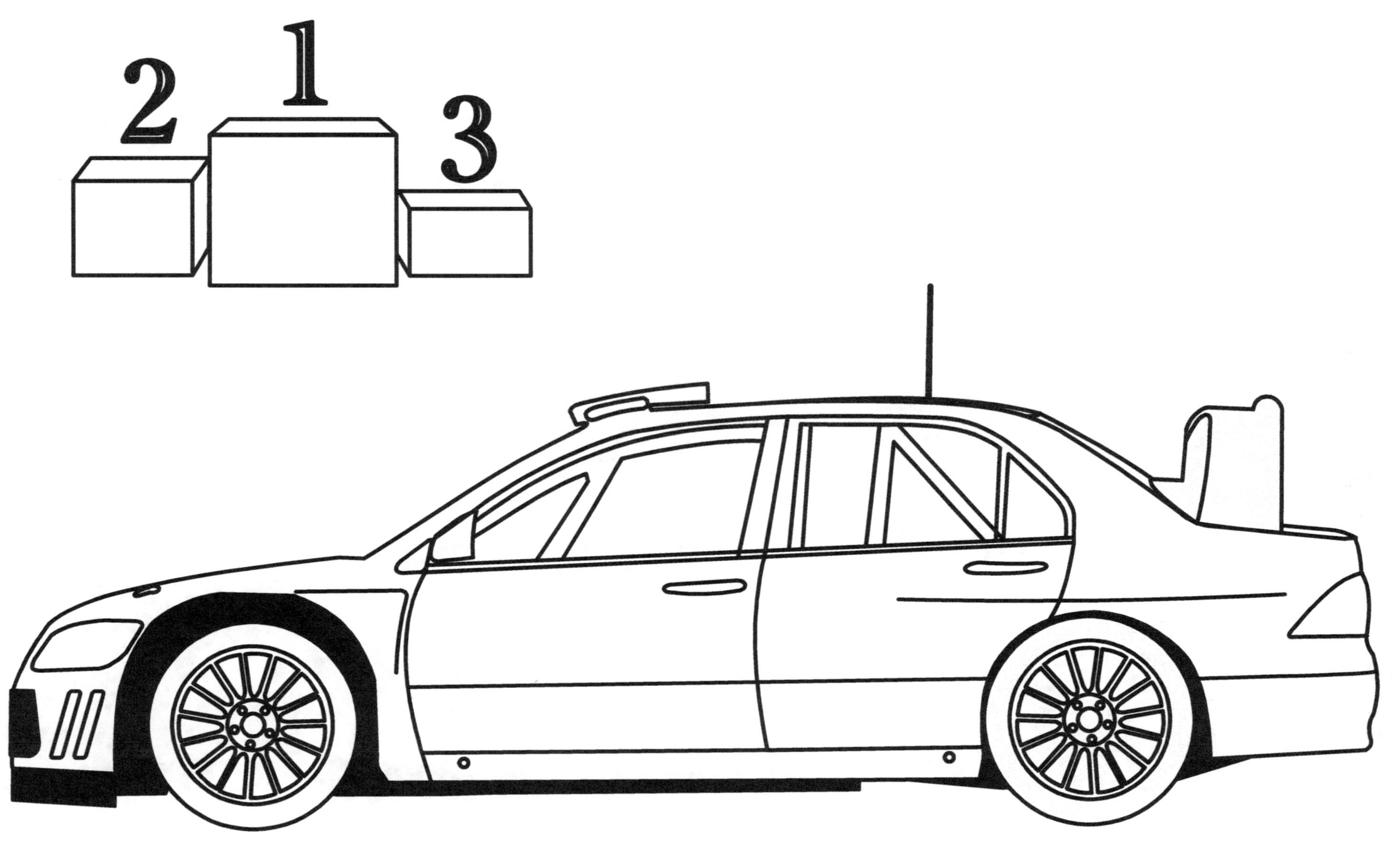

2
1
3

 # REPEAT 

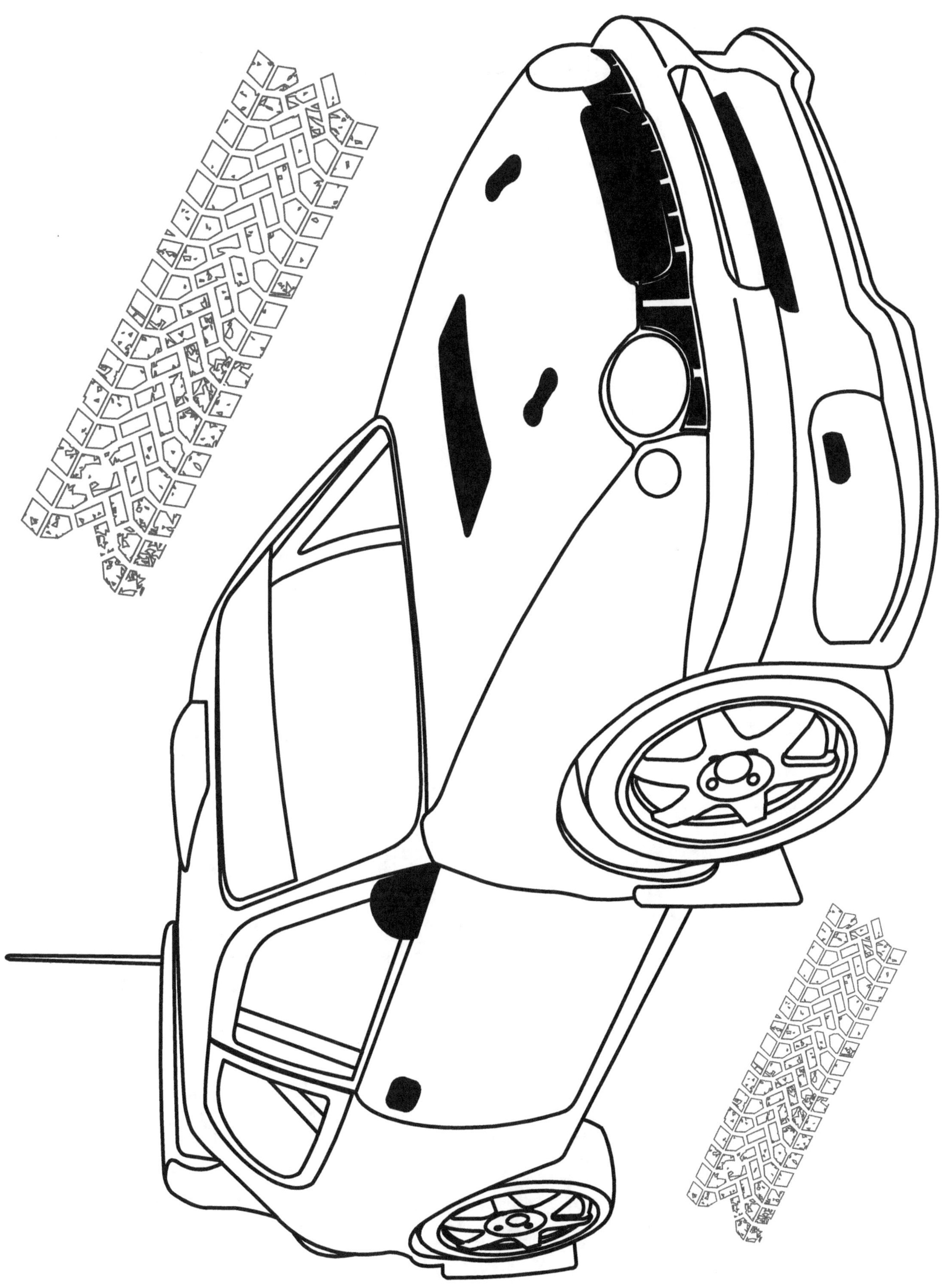

 # REPEAT 

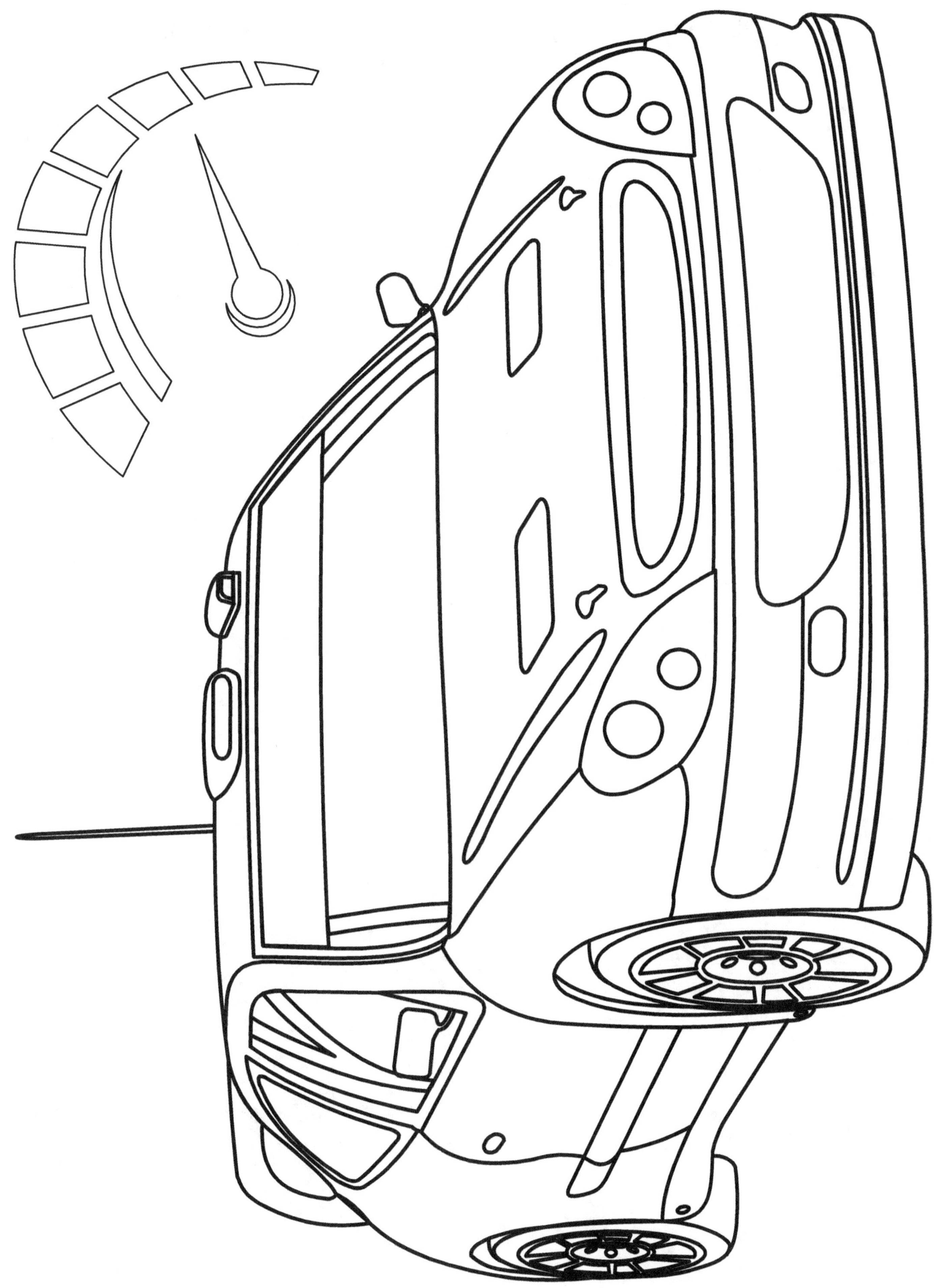

 # REPEAT 

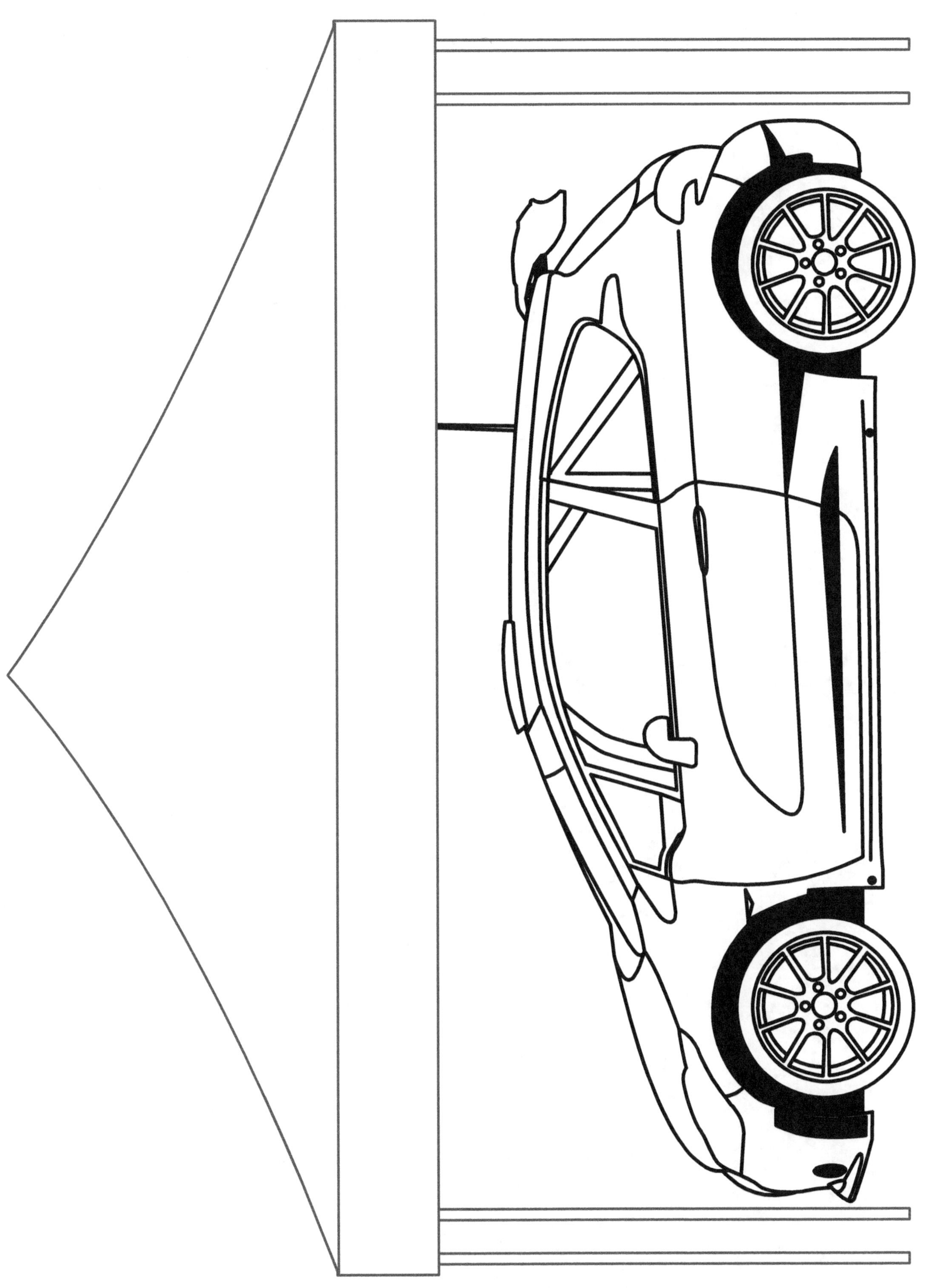

 # REPEAT 

 **REPEAT** 

GO !!!

 # REPEAT 

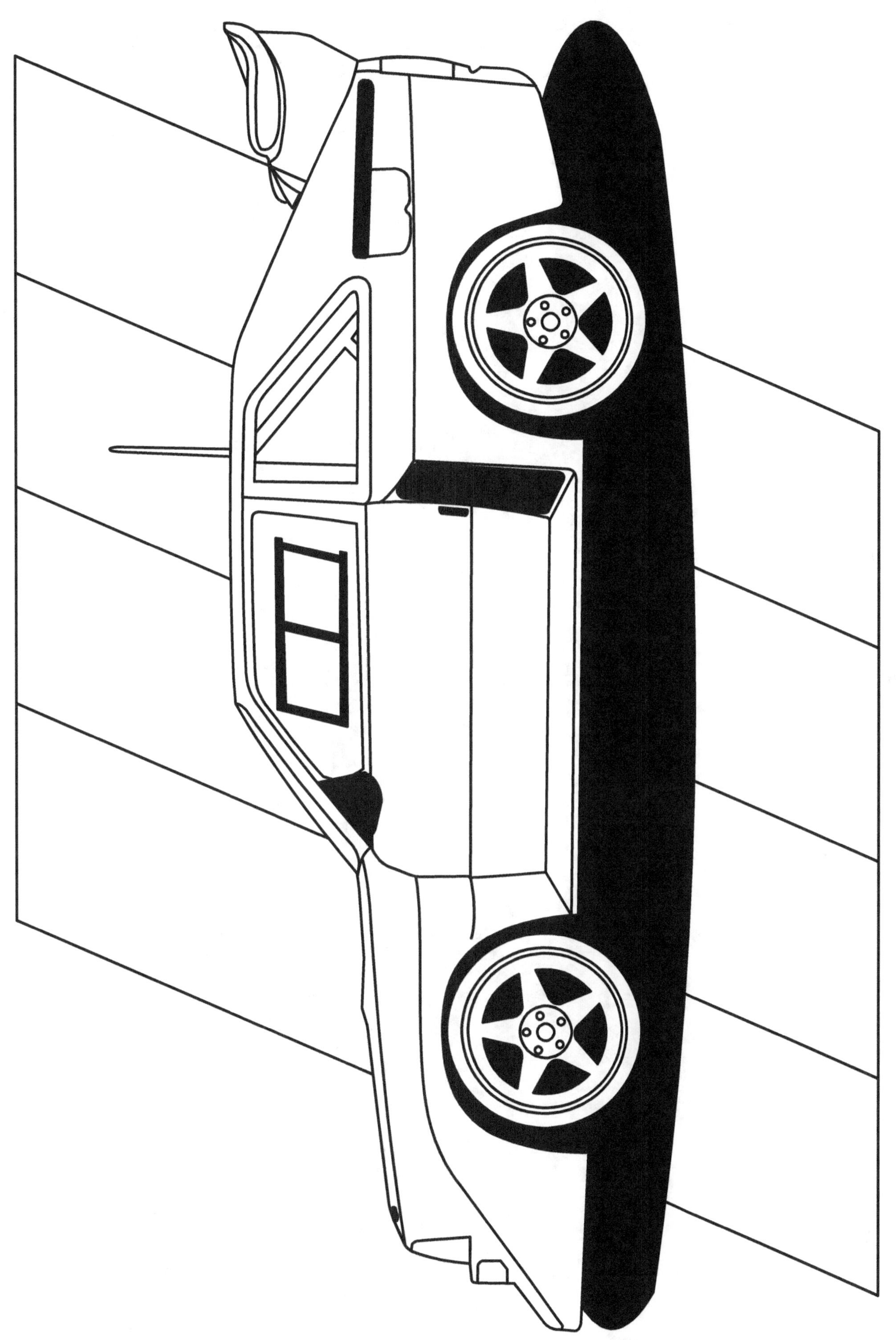

 # REPEAT 

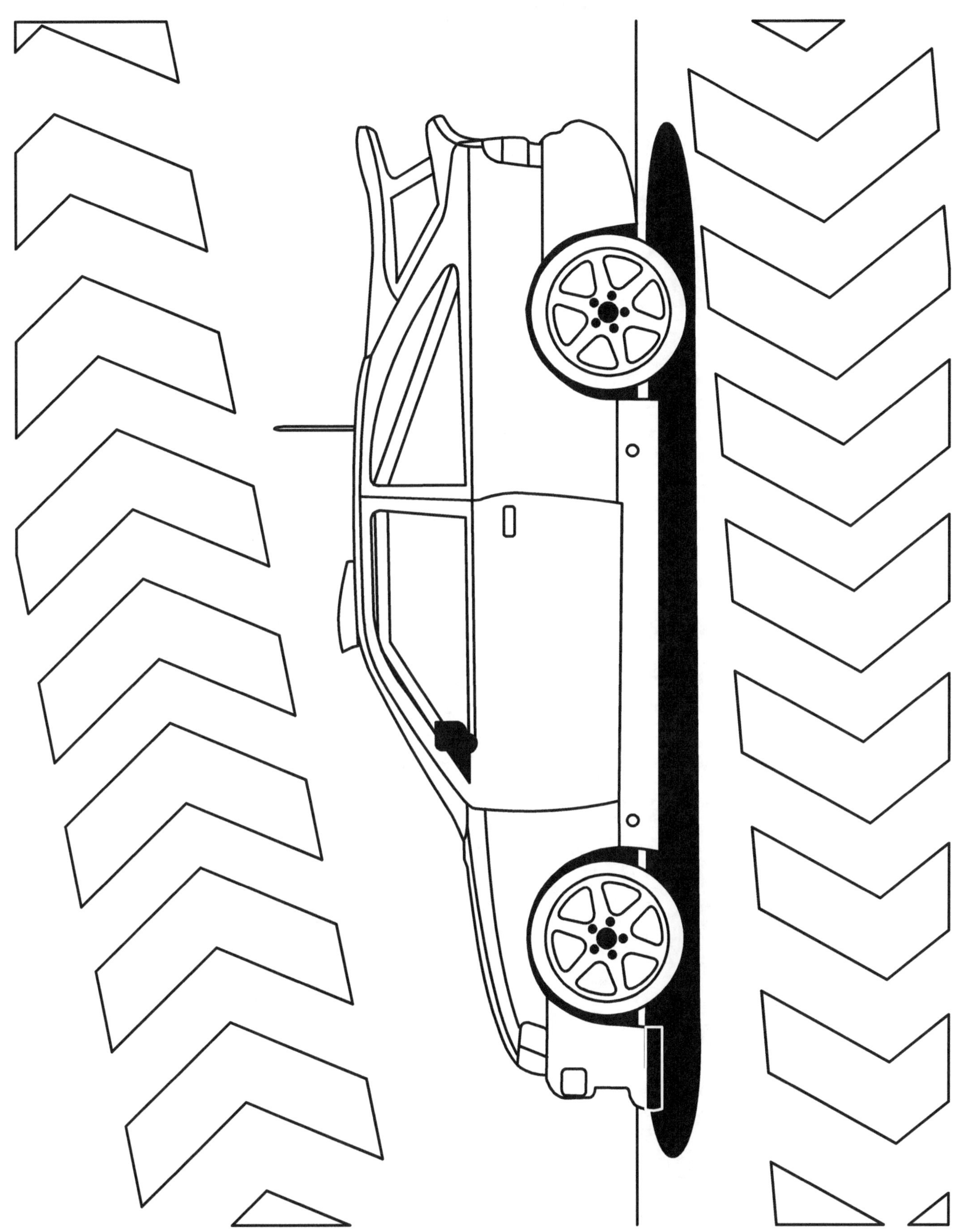

 # REPEAT 

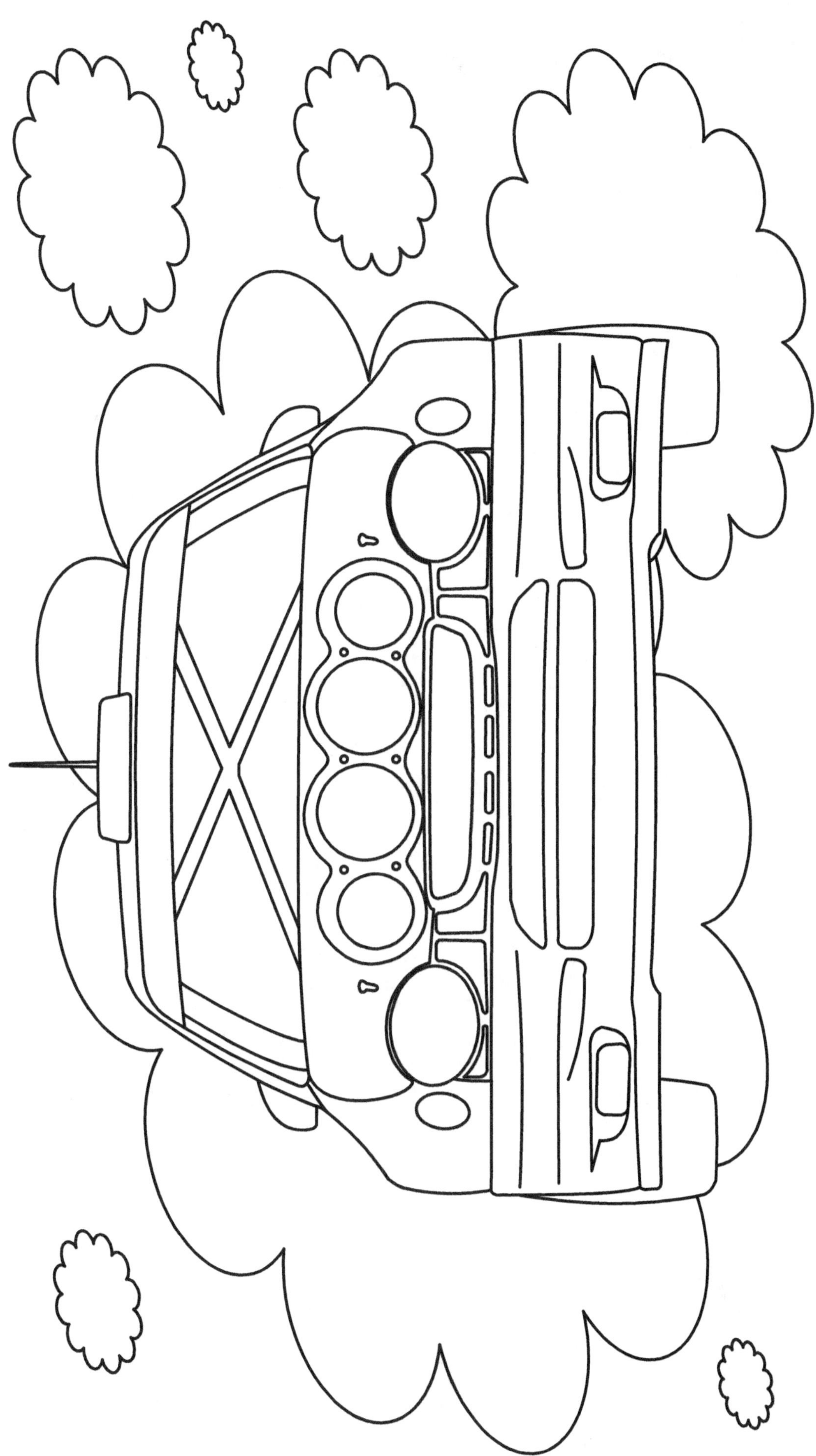

 REPEAT 

 # REPEAT 

 # REPEAT 

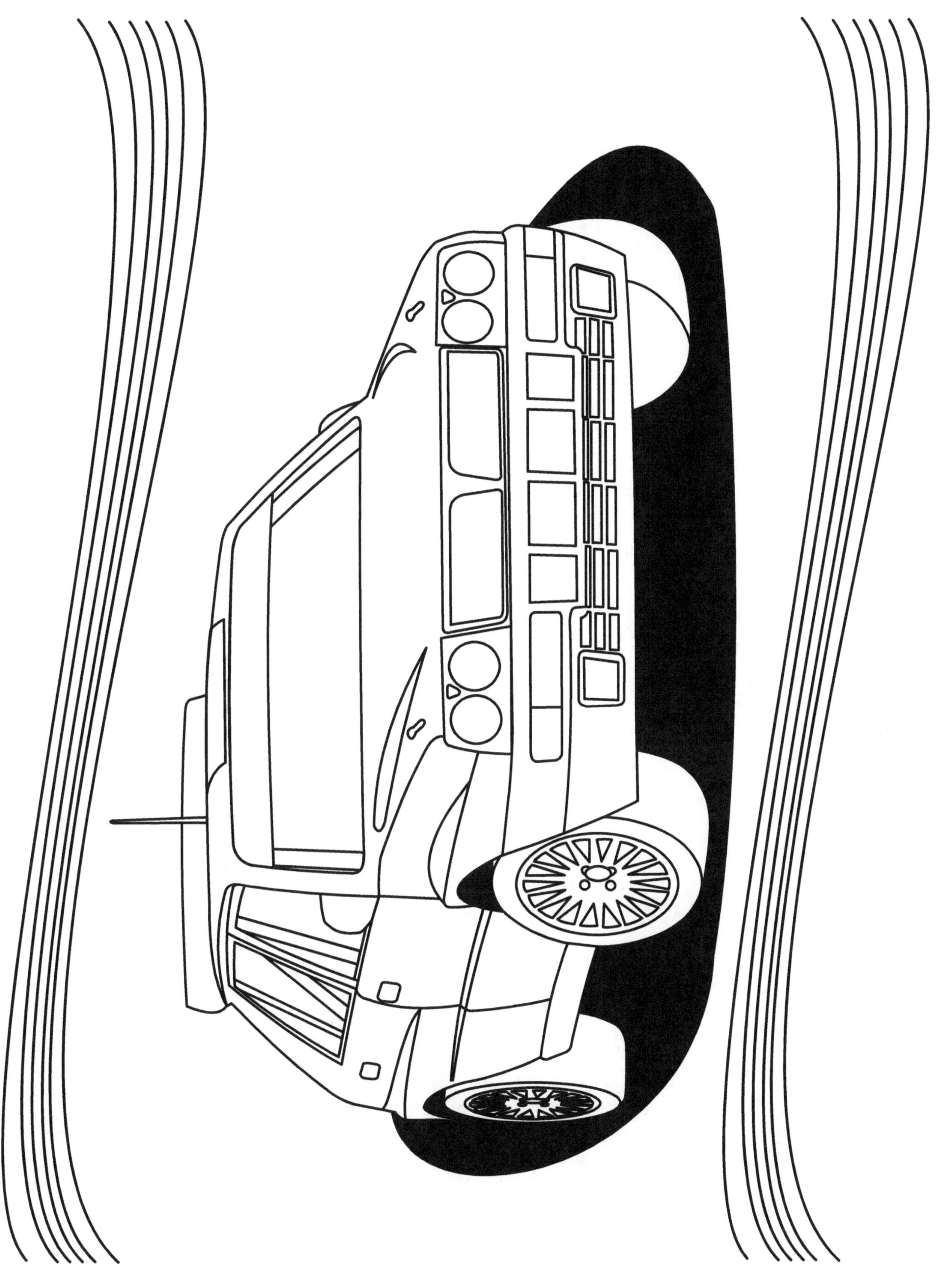

 # REPEAT 

R4c→90↑→HL2p
¡¡¡¡
2C↰6L-Hi
12015
80+80
H↑L3s
3R∧90∨HL2c
3R+4R-:)
6L+5Rc

 # REPEAT 

START

 # REPEAT 

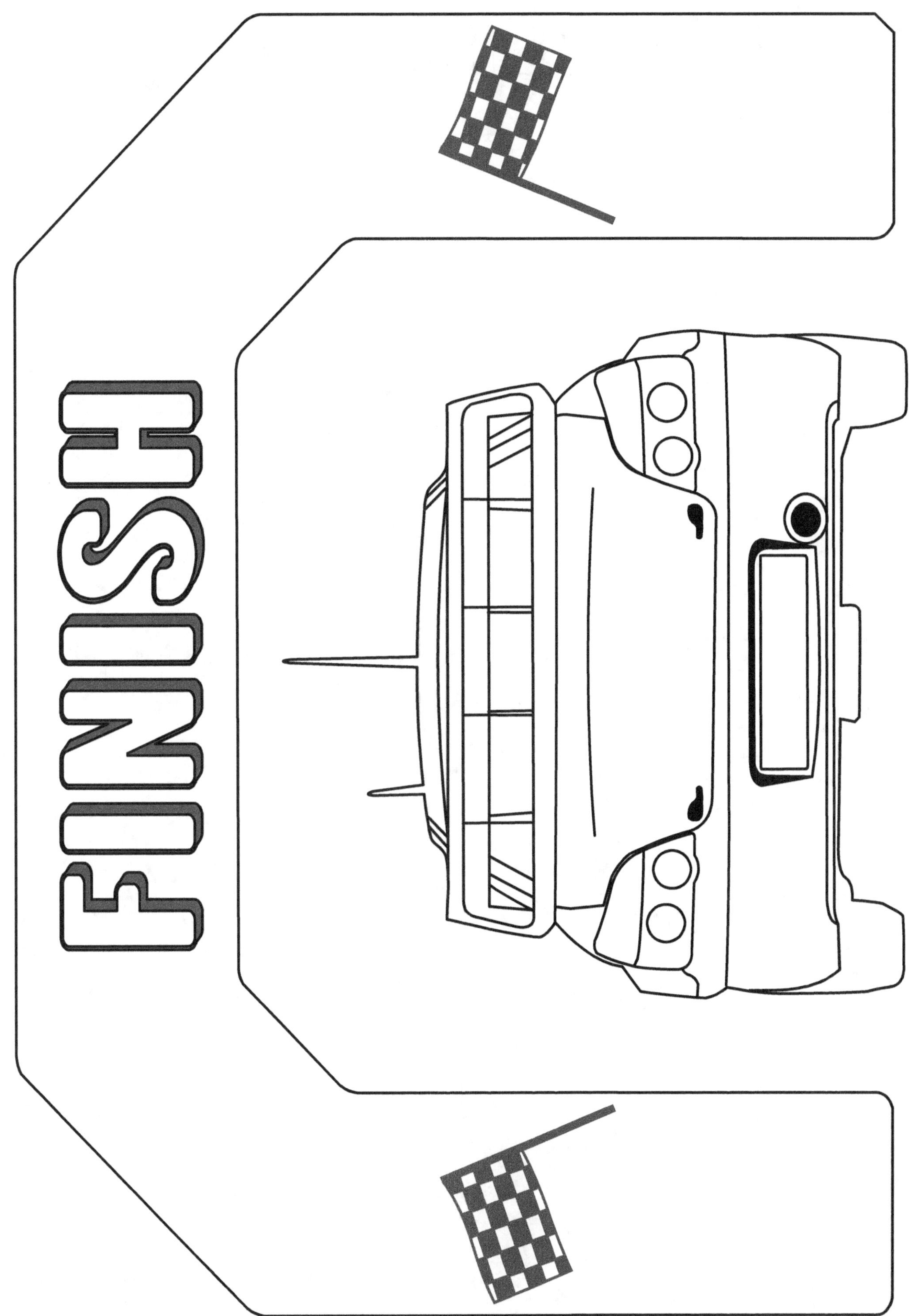
FINISH

 # REPEAT 

www.ingramcontent.com/pod-product-compliance
Lightning Source LLC
Chambersburg PA
CBHW080042260726
48658CB00007B/2703